THE
Solution
Focus
Handbook for Schools

Dawn Walters

Publisher Information

Copyright © 2013 Dawn Walters

For more information, or to contact the author, please email: wdawn19@gmail.com

Contents

THE
Solution
Focus

Handbook for Schools

Foreword

When I left the classroom 5 years ago, it was with great anticipation and hope that I approached my next job - working with the highest profile young people in schools. These children were disaffected and saw no reason to behave well or to want to succeed academically.

It took me several weeks into the new job however, to realize that what we were doing with these students, on the whole, wasn't working; target setting, anger management sessions, weeks out of main school spent in Behaviour Support Units[1]. The evidence was there. To look back through the files of some students I would find that they might have reached Year 11, but the problems they had in Year 1 were still there despite numerous interventions, often by several outside agencies. There were some successes and indeed some students, who came to the service in turmoil, left with a more positive attitude to school and adults.

I realized also the importance of working very closely with parents. Yes, many schools had written into their policies that they work very closely with parents. However, on many occasions this would simply involve sending letters home informing parents of misdemeanours, inviting parents into school to discuss misdemeanours, or inviting parents to

---

[1] BEHAVIOUR SUPPORT UNITS (known also as Pupil Referral Units): developed in certain parts of the country to accommodate pupils, who were not functioning in mainstream school, because they were experiencing difficulties with behaviour. However, if behaviour didn't improve students could still be excluded from a Behaviour Support Unit.

multi-agency[2] meetings. It must be pointed out, however, that many schools keep in frequent contact with parents to inform them of their children's very good performance or, indeed, improved performance.

At this point in the new job, I was still able to make home visits. So, using the skills from my Basic Certificate in Counselling, I did what I could to support parents with their children - I felt the support needed to be hands on. Parents appreciated these visits - often (for whatever reason) they found it an unhappy experience going into schools. So, these home visits helped but did not leave the results I was envisaging - happy parents, happy students and happy teachers.

Then one day at work we were informed that we were to receive a day's training in Solution Focus Brief Therapy from the most well-known practitioners in England, Brief. Admittedly, I viewed this training simply as a day off work, because, as many of you reading this will agree, after a day's training, the subject is often forgotten and notes filed under 'for the bin in a year's time'. Of course, you all know what happened next! I was completely bowled over by Solution Focus Brief Therapy (SFBT). I was excited that a procedure so simple could change a person's life in so few sessions. I was impressed with how it invited people to go into their imagination and to use this often untapped useful resource to harness their strengths - strengths they often did not realize they had or had forgotten they had. I was impressed too by its respectfulness: how it acknowledged a person's strengths and ability to cope no matter what

---

[2] MULTI-AGENCY MEETINGS: meetings at which several outside agencies are present to discuss ways forward for students experiencing difficulties. Parents and carers may be invited to attend these meetings.

situation they found themselves in. Most importantly for me, SFBT, through simple questioning and respectful collaborations with a person, is able to locate a person's innate resources and capitalize on them: "there's nothing that's wrong with you that what is right with you couldn't fix."

Other participants on the course were just as impressed but wrote it off making comments such, "nothing can be that wonderful," "it seems too good to be true, he's (Chris Iveson) just a good speaker." Others thought he was living in "cloud cuckoo land."

The next day in school, I launched into using what I had learned the day before. I discovered that although SFBT is simple, it's not easy - you have to get used to a completely new way of thinking: being solution-focused instead of problem-focused. You have to get used to the idea that your role is not to give advice but to support the person to find their own best advice for themselves. You have to notice resources your client has and comment on these. So, using what I had gleaned from a day's course I set forth.

Unbelievably, I received a 'phone-call a few days after that first session from a Head of Year asking me what I had done to D---! My immediate reaction was that D--- had gone completely off the rails and that this 'phone-call was a complaint. I listened further. D--- was behaving well. Instead of truanting during lessons, he was in lessons. He was doing his work, he was arriving on time and he was in full school uniform. The Head of Year remained bemused. I therefore gave him more details about the SFBT technique. I explained to him how D--- had expected to tell me about the naughty things he had been up to in school and how he thought I had been called in to tell him how to improve. I pointed out to the Head of Year that this was NOT what SFBT was about. I told him how I had explained to D--- that I was more interested in hearing from him what his life would look like when the problem was gone. Having established this from D---, I found out from him how he would achieve these goals. I pointed out to the Head of Year that often this first small step can create a domino effect and therefore could create a greater impact than expected.

We ended our conversation with the Head of Year intent on arranging SFBT training for the school's Learning Mentors and Teaching Assistants. I suggested the teachers would benefit from the training too!

After this 'phone-call I became 100 percent committed to SFBT. I read copious books on the subject and attended as many courses as I could. Here was another successful tool that could be added to the workbox of those striving to support young people in schools.

Interestingly, what turned out to be the solution for a lot of students was frequently quite unexpected. There is a saying in the SFBT world that: 'the solution to the problem is often not what we expect it to be.'

Apart from happier teachers and happier students, one of the biggest groups of beneficiaries is the parents. Finally, they were approached in a consistently respectful manner. What they were able to do well was recognised. How they wanted theirs and their children's lives to look - it was acknowledged. There was no hint of them being considered bad and responsible for the ills of society: they felt they were being listened to and being supported. This in itself broke down many barriers between school and home - the 'them and us' barrier. At this point I return to the present. I return to the reason for writing this book.

Imagine you've been suffering from a complaint for a long time and then by some chance you discover that there's an excellent medicine out there that remedies the complaint. Only thing is this medicine's so simple, so cheap and has been available in your local chemists for years. Imagine your relief yet surprise - or even disbelief.

This is how I regard SFBT and schools. SFBT is used with massive success in Business, Drugs and Alcohol Rehabilitation and Mental Health Settings amongst many others. Nowhere, in my opinion, however, does its productive effect touch the soul as much as when you see a troubled child (and often their family) return to happiness.

I believe every school would benefit from having SFBT as one of its helping tools. I hope this manual inspires those who read it to at least test the waters.

Dawn Walters, *March 2013*

There is nothing wrong with you that what is right with you couldn't fix.

Early Intervention

The recent launch of the Early Intervention Strategy in some cities has caused many to breathe a sigh of relief. Finally, government has realised that it is far more economical to deal with the causes of problems in our society rather than to deal with the outcomes. It is more economical on both a human level and a financial level. If we can support people earlier, when we see signs of a problem, then we possibly save those people and others in their immediate families and communities from unnecessary pain and upset. It follows then that early financial intervention must be 'good housekeeping': the time taken for a school to speak with the parents/carers of a child who is exhibiting concerning behaviour and then to point them in the right direction for support could turn out to be an excellent investment. This could be the action that stops this student spiralling out of control and finding themselves on the well-trodden route of exclusion from school to incarceration - it is cheaper to work with a family immediately when it encounters problems than to pay for the subsequent outcomes if they are not supported.

Solution Focus could have a powerful role to play in Early Intervention - especially in schools. Because of its non-intrusive, respectful and supportive qualities, many students and their families feel safer and less emotionally exposed accessing help from others when this method is used.

How to use this manual

There are many tools in Solution Focus and as you become more familiar with the method you will become better at choosing the most appropriate one for a given situation.

Whilst the list of tools is set out in a possible order in which they might be used during a standard solution focus session, please note that this does not imply the order in which you have to use them.

Each situation will require its own tools (questions) and that will be up to you to decide what should logically come next in order to support this student/person.

I would recommend, however, that you always establish a goal and that you always, where possible, strive to discover any positive pre-meeting changes and to establish how the student managed to make these changes; follow this by cheerleading the role the student played in making these positive changes happen.

Having been a teacher myself in several busy comprehensives, I am all too aware of the time constraints on teachers: rushing from one lesson to the next; signing report cards at the end of lessons; break-time and lunchtime duties; lunchtime meetings; meetings with parents before school, at lunchtime and after school; staff meetings; year team meetings; faculty meetings; house meetings; planning meetings; SEN meetings; and the list goes on without lesson planning and marking even being mentioned!

Bearing in mind the small amount of time teachers have left over in their working week, I designed the lay-out of this manual to cater for the busy teacher.

Instead of a lengthy description of each tool, I have given an example conversation demonstrating the tool being used by a teacher in a school. This shortens the reading and learning time for the teacher/user, because the example is the explanation and teachers can see the tool at work straight-away in a typical school situation.

The book also includes other uses and ideas in school of SFBT: Becoming a solution focused school; Solution Focus Pictures; the Solution Focus Multi-agency Meeting and Group Solution Focus Work.

Loads of reasons why Solution Focus works in schools

- It is solution-focused!
- It is brief.
- It is hopeful and possibility-oriented.
- It is respectful.
- It seeks out a student's resources.
- It uses those resources to support the student to move forward.
- It finds the student's strengths and praises them.
- It allows the student to go into his/her imagination.
- It supports the student towards solutions.
- It understands that the solution to a problem is often not what we expect it to be.
- It finds out what the student wants to happen.
- It measures how much the student wants things to improve and how willing he/she is to do this.
- It acknowledges and 'cheerleads' improvements.
- It allows the student to identify when support will no longer be needed.
- It treats the student as the expert in all aspects of their lives.
- It detects the times when the problem might be ABSENT and seeks to increase these.

The
solution focused
method seeks out a
self healing or self
actualising drive by
actively focussing on
strengths and
resources.

The Tools

- Problem Free Talks
- Pre-session Change
- The Goal
- Miracle Question
- Reframing from the absence of something to the presence of something.
- Exceptions
- How Possible
- Scaling
- Acknowledging Strengths
- What else?
- How, What, Who, Where – Never Why
- Just Suppose
- You must have a very good reason
- How will you know?
- Reciprocal Effects
- Flagging the Minefield
- My proudest Achievement
- Cheerleading
- Homework

Problem-free Talk 1

In order to achieve the best outcome from a session it is important to form a rapport between you and the student.

I have found that students are willing to engage in problem-free talk if the adult talks about him/herself first.

When I don't know the student I simply tell them my hobbies and interest, that I have 2 children, their ages, what they are into. I then tell them my favourite film, favourite music, favourite actor, favourite food etc. Next, I proceed to find out the same information from the student, stopping along the way sometimes to make a comment on something the student has said. For example, one girl chose macaroni cheese as her favourite food. I pointed out that that was also my daughter's favourite food and that we had it weekly on Mondays. I could have also told her that my daughter loves it so much that she's learned to make it herself and now cooks it for the whole family giving me a night off from cooking.

The teacher, who is more acquainted with a student may ask about a student's favourite things and also probably will know other information about the student, such as numbers of brothers and sisters, football team the student supports, any clubs the student attends in school, any subject the student excels in or has begun to excel in school.

IT CAN BE VERY USEFUL FOR THE TEACHER TO BE ARMED WITH PROBLEM-FREE INORMATION IN ORDER TO ENGAGE IN PROBLEM-FREE TALK. OF COURSE, YOU CAN STILL ENGAGE WITHOUT PRIOR INFORMATION.

As mentioned earlier, if you are able to, it could be highly beneficial to the student to give something of yourself. This breaks clown barriers and may help the student to relax.

The aim of problem-free talk is to set the scene. To announce that this session is not about blaming, shaming or threats etc. It is a respectful session, where 2 interested parties will collaborate to look at the possibilities of changing or improving things.

Example Conversation

When the student speaks to someone outside of school, e.g. a behaviour support teacher from the local authority children's department.

"Hi. My name is Helen and I am the Behaviour Support Teacher for this school. I visit several other schools in this area. Thank you for agreeing to see me. I would like to just tell you something about myself so you don't wonder who this stranger is. So, I have 2 children, who are 18 and 12. My hobbies are reading, gardening and writing. My favourite meals are lasagne and curries. My favourite colours are blue and purple. My favourite film is Pretty Woman. My favourite subject when I was at school was German. I support Chelsea Football Club. Now you know something about me, I would like to find out a little about you."

What are your hobbies, what do you enjoy doing in your spare time?

What's your favourite meal?

Favourite colour?

Favourite film?

Favourite subject in school?

Do you support a football team?

You will find that, although you are simply asking a list of questions, a dialogue will ensue as you show interest in the student's replies and engage with them.

"What are your hobbies?"
"Playing out and computers"

"Where do you play out?"
"At the 'wreck' behind the estate."

"Oh, I've heard of the 'wreck', some of the students from another school were telling me about it. It sounds like a popular place. What sort of computers are you into?"
"I mean computer games really and I like playing them on the PS3."

"What's your favourite meal?"
"Pizza."

"Any particular type?"
"Just cheese and tomato."

"Favourite colour?"
"Red."

"That's not the colour of your football team is it?"
"Yes."

"Favourite football team?"
"Charlton"

"They'll be as great as Chelsea one day!"
"Yeah, we're poor and Chelsea's got loads of money, they SHOULD be great."

"Point taken. Favourite film?"
"I've got too many. I can't think of just one."

"If you were stranded on a desert island and you could only take one, which one would you choose? I'm really pushing you to choose."
"Saving Private Ryan."

"Wow! That's a really deep, thoughtful and thought-provoking film. You must be a person, who is quite thoughtful."
"Yeah, sometimes."

Problem-free talk 2

(when the student talks to a permanent member of school staff)

In this conversation, James, the student, is talking to his Head of Year, Mr Jones.

"Hi James, we've only got 25 minutes to talk, because I'll be teaching after that. I see Charlton lost again this week. Do you think they'll get relegated?"
"Definitely, it they don't start doing better."

"They'd do better if they had more money to spend, perhaps. Anyway James, take a seat over there. I thought it might be useful if you came to see me this morning for a chat."

"What do you suppose I want to talk about?"
"My behaviour."

"I don't really know that much about what's been happening. So, would you like something to be different about your behaviour?"

A short solution focused exchange will ensue with James telling Mr Jones that he wants to do better in History. Mr Jones will help James find a way to do this by enquiring of him how he's managing to keep things going well in other areas and by wondering whether James is able to transfer some of those skills. He leaves James with a first step towards this task. This first step consists of James simply borrowing a behaviour from another lesson. In this case it is sitting with the girls away from the boys. In the short time they have Mr Jones scales James on his commitment to change.

Pre-session change

Find out from the student what has improved since they knew this session was planned.

This gives the adult the opportunity to give ownership to the student for any small step forward.

It also allows the adult to cheerlead. Example

Conversation

"So, what's improved with you since you knew you were having this session with me?"
"I don't know."

"Just suppose you knew."
"I've started getting to some of my lessons on time."

"You're getting to some of your lessons on time! Wow! How are you managing to do that?"
"Instead of hanging around talking to my mates, I'm starting to go straight to my next lesson."

"That must be hard leaving your mates."
"Yes, but when I get to lessons on time I get a good report and a 'phone-call home. Mum likes that."

"That's really impressive! You are so keen to do well that you ignore your mates sometimes and get to the lesson on time and then you know that pleases your

mum. You obviously think a lot of your mum to do this. You're a thoughtful person. Did you know that?"

"No, not really."

"This is great, you've done this yourself. Nobody made you do it. You've decided for yourself that you like the results of being on time for your lessons."

"I suppose so."

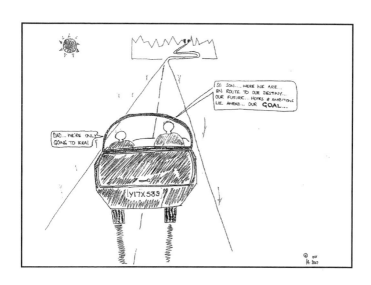

If you keep doing what you've always done, you'll get what you've always got.

The Goal

Example Conversation

"So, thank you for agreeing to see me today. What would need to be different in your life after these sessions for you to feel it was worth seeing me?"
"Things would be better in school. I'd be behaving. My behaviour would be different, really."

NOTE:

You may get the response: "I don't understand the question."

You could re-phrase the question.

Re-phrasing the question:

"What would you like to be different and better in your life after these sessions?"

OR

"How might I be able to help you today?"

If, after re-phrasing the question the student has no answer, go straight to the Miracle Question

REMEMBER: You don't even need to know what the problem is to work with someone.

TOOLS
The Miracle Question

Gives the student the opportunity to imagine life without the problem.

Example Conversation

"You go to bed tonight and while you are sleeping a miracle happens. You didn't cause it to happen – it just happens. When you wake up in the morning, you know things are different. You know life is exactly as you want it to be. What is the first sign that things have changed for the better?"
"I open my eyes and instead of feeling down, I yawn and stretch and jump out of bed. My mum calls up, "Darren, get out of bed sweetheart" instead of what she normally says, "Get up, you lazy little sod". I go downstairs and my breakfast is on the table and my mum is smiling at me. She kisses me on the forehead and tells me to enjoy my breakfast. Normally, she slaps me around the head and tells me how bad I am for getting up late."

"What else?"
"Well, normally I hang around with the other kids 'till I'm late. But on this morning, I go straight to school, go into school and head to my classroom. All the teachers smile at me and say, "Good morning". Normally they find some reason for telling me off and never say hello, let alone smile"

"What else?"
"When I get into class I do my work instead of messing about as usual. The teacher tells me I have been good and I get a good message in my diary. My mum reads it at the end of the day and she is really pleased, so I don't get grounded like I normally do"

This conversation can then be continued by using the following tools:

- How Possible
- Scaling

The conversation might continue in this manner:

"How possible is it for this Miracle to happen?"
"Very possible"

"On a scale of 1 – 10, 1 being it is impossible and 10 being it could happen if I wanted it to, how much do you want this to happen?"
"9"

"Wow! That's quite high."

The teacher can then explore further by finding out when any of the miracle happened in the past and what was different when it happened. The conversation could continue thus:

"When has any of the Miracle happened in the past, even if just a little bit?"
"Well, about 2 years ago when I was in Year 7, I used to get up on time and arrive at school on time and everything was ok."

"Wow! So, what was different then?"

"Well, when my dad lived with us, he used to take my Playstation off me at 9.00 and make me go to bed. I used to be asleep by probably 9.30. Now, I just play until I fall asleep and that is often at about 3 am"

"OK, so now you are getting a lot less sleep!"

Reframing from the absence of something to the presence of something/instead.

This tool is very powerful in starting to change someone's mindset from a negative one to a positive. It gives people the opportunity to see what their desired future will look like.

Example Conversation.

Darren is with his parents and his Year Head at a meeting, where his lack of homework is being discussed.

"So Darren, you were about to tell us what would have to happen for you to start being polite and behaving well in lessons."
"The teachers would have to stop shouting at me."

"What would they be doing instead?"
"They would speak to me nicely in a kind way and would smile when they are talking to me."

"What else?"
"The teachers would stop expecting me to understand everything straightaway like all the boffins in the class."

"What would happen instead of this?"
"They would walk 'round the class and help us while we are doing the exercises. They would ask us who needs help and tell us to put our hands up so that they or the teaching assistant could help us."

"What else?"
"The teachers wouldn't just sit at their desks on the computers or writing things at their desks."

"What would happen instead?"
"Like before, they would get up and come and see us and help us."

Exceptions

This tool is used when the teacher/counsellor wants the student to identify a time/occasion when the problem doesn't exist. Once this occasion has been identified, the teacher/counsellor then explores with the student what is different at these times – why does the problem not happen at these times, or why does the student not notice the problem at these times.

Example conversation

"So Dawn, when are the times you are not nervous on the aeroplane?"
"Well, I'm not always nervous on the plane, it's just at the beginning. I take some time to settle down and think I might even panic."

"So, when are the times at the beginning of the flight when you don't feel this way?"
"I've noticed that when I take a magazine with me, I settle down quite easily and really get into the magazine."

"What sort of magazines do you take on the flight?"
"Gossipy ones. Like "Heat" and 'Now'."

"You like gossip do you?"
"I must do! I thought that myself! I didn't realize until just now!"

"So, what's different when you are reading a magazine, a gossipy one?"
"I forget what's going on around me and get into all the scandal on the pages. I also love fashion and there's loads about fashion in these magazines. I just feel relaxed, I suppose, and don't think about anything bad anymore."

"When are other times you don't feel fearful?"
"When I have a seat that's spacious. Like the door seats, or the seats at the back near the toilets where there's loads of room. I don't feel so trapped then, not so hemmed in."

"Ok Dawn. That's brilliant. You know some ways of allowing yourself to be calm. I want you to keep doing these things, because they are working for you. During the next few days, when you get a chance, I want you to think of other times when you are happy and relaxed while flying."

How possible is it?

This tool enables the teacher/counsellor to support the student in gauging the possibility of action by themselves and/or other people in their lives.

Example Conversation

"Hi John, thank you for coming to see me. I know things have been difficult in your Biology class with Mrs Kennedine. She asked me to speak to you. I wonder if you would tell me more about what is happening."
"Me and Mrs Kennedine just do not get on. She thinks I am a trouble maker and a bad person, just because I know all the answers and I stand up to her. How can she keep on giving me detentions? It's not fair."

"Mrs Kennedine recognizes there is a problem and she would like to come to a solution. How possible is it that you will work with us to sort this out?"
"Very possible."

"Great. How possible on a scale of 1 – 10, 1 being it is so possible, it will probably happen?"
"10."

"Wow! So you really do want this to happen!"
"Yes."

Scaling 1

Example Conversation

"So, you mean to turn things around in lessons by: paying attention to the teacher, doing your work, joining in the lesson, answering questions, putting your hand up and asking for help and keeping away from the boys you normally mess around with."
"Yes."

"That's great! How committed are you to making this happen? On a scale of 0 -10, 0 = I don't think I can make it happen at all and 10 = I am absolutely certain I can and I will."
"8"

"Wow! That's high! How come? What' already happening that's made it an 8?"
"Because I've done it before so I know I can do it and I want to get better reports."

"What else?"
"I want to get better grades so I can move up into higher groups. I need 5 GCSEs to get into college to do Graphics."

"Oh wow! You want to do Graphics!"
"Yes, it's my favourite subject."

"I can believe 13that - you seem very determined to get to college to study it."

Scaling 2

You may find that, as opposed to the example in Scaling 1, the student chooses a much lower figure....

Example Conversation

(from a group of Year 10 students on the verge of exclusion in a large comprehensive).

"So, Maryann, just suppose you knew what the reason might be for you being invited by the Deputy Head Teacher to join this group?"
"'Cos my behaviour is crap. I don't go to lessons, I smoke in the breaktimes and when I do go to lessons I swear at the teachers. I just tell them to f--- off if they annoy me!"

"Let me ask you an interesting question. On a scale of 0 to 10, 0 being my behaviour is absolutely rubbish and 10 being my behaviour is brilliant, where would you place yourself on this scale?"
"0.5"

"Ok. You could have said 0, where has the .5 come from? What's happening that's good to make you give yourself that extra .5?"
"Well, I'm not bad in all my lessons. I go to the lessons where the teachers aren't cheeky to me, and if they show me respect then I show them respect back."

"Sounds fair to me. Maryann, I have to say I am impressed with your honesty, it's really nice to meet someone like you. Now, how will you know that your score has moved up to 1?"

"I'd start going to more lessons."

"What else?"

"I'd go to school more."

"Right. You'd go to school more. What difference would it make to you if you went to school more?"

"Then I would get some GCSEs, especially Art then I could go to college."

"Wow! You're an artist - I've always liked the idea of designing my own clothes but I can still only draw stick people. So, you need to come to school in order to get some qualifications."

"Yes, but the teachers get on my nerves."

"On a scale of 0 - 10, 0 being I don't want it at all and 10 being I would really love it to happen, how much would you want to come to school and be happy here?"

"10."

Acknowledging Strengths and Successes

Example Conversation

"So, it's been 2 weeks since we last spoke. It's nice to meet you again. What's improved since we last met?"
"Don't know."

"Just suppose you did know?"
"Well, I haven't had any bad letters home."

"What else?"
"I've been behaving in all my lessons."

"What else?"
"I'm getting higher marks."

"What else?"
"My mum's so pleased with me that she's upped my pocket money."

"Wow! Impressive. So you've been behaving well in your lessons and your marks have improved. It's no wonder your mum's so proud of you! How did you manage to do all this?"
"In lessons, I did what I said I'd do: I've kept away from the friends I used to get in trouble with. So, I'm concentrating more and just getting my work done. I want to move up into a higher group."

"You really do want to move up a set don't you! I am really impressed with how you've stuck to your guns and kept away from your friends even though it would be more fun. You have great determination. When you mean to do something you do it, don't you? You get things done. Your mum's trust in you must have increased. She must think now, 'Dwayne does what he says he's going to do.'"

Do something different

What Else?

Example Conversation.

"So, instead of messing about in class you'd be paying attention to the teacher and doing your work. What else?"
"I'd be joining in the lesson answering questions and putting my hand up."

"What else?"
"I'd sit away from the boys I normally mess around with."

"What else?"
"I'd put my hand up and ask for help if I got stuck instead of just chatting."

This simple technique is extremely effective in increasing the opportunity for students to 'dig deep' and discover more resources within themselves, possibilities they might not have considered otherwise. As they continue to respond to the 'what else' question, they are also in the process of creating a new picture of their life - an alternative new positive image of life.

How, What, Who, Where – Never Why

Example Conversation

"Who else has noticed this determination?"
"My teachers."

"How do you know that they've noticed?"
"Their attitudes towards me have changed."

"What have they said?"
"They are treating me with more respect, treating me in a more mature way."

"Where have you noticed this the most?"
"In the lessons where I'm behaving the best - the teachers seem to like me more and have a joke with me."

"How will you know that things are continuing to improve?"
"I'll keep on getting on well with the teachers and one of them will say, I'm moving you up to a higher set!"

"What would other members of your family say if they could see you in school now?"
"They'd be shocked and surprised but they would be proud of me."

"Who would be the most proud?"

"My nan (gran). She'd say 'at last you're making your mum's life easier, good lad.'"

Just Suppose

"What's changed? What's better since I last saw you?"
"I'm out of the Referral Unit now and back in my lessons. I am doing as the teachers ask me, speaking politely to everyone."

"Wow! How did you manage all that?"
"I don't know."

"Just suppose you did know!"
"I've just been doing as the teachers tell me straight away and when I do this they treat me better, like they ring my mum and tell her and she's kinder to me then."

NOTE: We use 'just suppose' when the student seems stuck and their only answer is, 'I don't know'. This is to give the student a gentle push. It takes the pressure off the student and moves away from direct action yet allows the student to use their imagination without committing themselves to anything.

If the student continues to answer with 'I don't know' you can then progress to asking, 'just suppose I asked someone who knew you really well how you did it, what would they say?'. Before asking this question, establish from the student who it is who knows him/her really well.

You must have a very good reason for....What is it?

Example Conversation

"What's better in school?"
"I listened to everything people said to me at the re-admission meeting two weeks ago and a lot of things have changed. My mum's been happy with me - Mr. Scott rings my mum up and tells her good things about me. But I'm still fibbing and that gets on people's nerves."

"You must have a very good reason for fibbing, what is it?"
"I enjoy trying to get away with it."

Once the 'very good reason' has been established, we can now go ahead and explore this very important information using other SF tools to move the student on.

Possible Conversation

"Wow! You are very brave taking such risks! As you have said though, your mum's happy with the changes you've already made. How much would you like to do something about the fibbing?"
"0 = not at all and 10 = a lot."
"8"

"That's high. How come you want this to change so much?"

"I'm fed up of getting caught out then getting into trouble."

"What will be your first small step towards changing this?"

"I'm going to make my screensaver on my 'phone into a message that says: 'tell the truth', then I will always be getting a reminder that will stick in my head even when I'm not at the computer."

How will you know?

This tool asks the student to find evidence to support changes that he/she expects to do/see.

Example Conversation

"So Katherine, you say that you will be behaving better in class. How will you know that things are improving?"
"The teacher will tell me, "well done" and she will smile at me instead of giving me dirty looks. I will get positive comments in my diary and my parents will be pleased with me. Best of all, I won't be missing my breaks and lunchtimes. Oh, and even better than that, NO MORE DETENTIONS!"

"You say your parents will be pleased with you. How will you know?"
"My mum will hug me when I get in because she will have received a 'phone-call from school telling me there is a great comment in my diary. She'll tell me that if I keep it up I will get a reward from her."

"Such as?"
"Extra pocket money, a new computer game or we get to have a girly night together."

Reciprocal Effects/What difference would it make?

This tool discovers what impact a person's changed behaviour will have on others. It puts the person in a position where they have to think about and ponder on other people's feelings.

Example conversation

"OK Celia. Your mum has rung the school and I know she is very upset about the recent note in your diary about you picking on younger students and making them and their families very unhappy, as a result. I know you have told your form teacher you want things to change. So, just suppose you did stop picking on younger girls, what difference would it make to your mum?"
"My mum would be able to relax, because she wouldn't always be worrying about a 'phone call from school, telling her bad things about me."

"What difference would your mum being relaxed make to you?"
"We would get on better. We would spend more time together chatting and having a laugh. We would watch TV together."

"What else?"
"I would probably get more things, extra pocket money."

"So, you are being kinder to the other girls. What difference would this make to your teachers?"
"They would be nicer to me. They would trust me and pick me for important jobs."

"What difference would it make to you when the teachers are being kinder to you?"
"I would feel like something. I would feel like I am worth something, like I am worth knowing."

Flagging the Minefield

Example Conversation

"So, sometimes even when we want to do well it can get difficult. So, you know all the things you want to do in lessons that will keep you on the right side of the teachers and therefore help to move you up into the higher sets."

"Yes."

"Just suppose then, on some occasions, in some lessons say, you find yourself slipping back into the bad habits. For example, in one lesson, you might say to yourself that, "I will just sit with my old friends today" or "Miss is too busy, I won't bother asking for help today because she won't notice me, I'll just chat to my friends." That sort of scenario. How are you going to make sure you don't start going down the slippery slope again?"

"I'll just think about all the bad things that could happen and that'd make me do the right thing. I'll just think, "if I start having a laugh with my friends it'll be fun, but I don't want another detention or a bad letter home." Plus, the teacher will probably think I would mess about in a higher class and spoil it for the brighter ones. Then I more than likely won't get moved up a set, which is what I want to happen."

A well-timed, genuine framing of a person's strengths can do more good than a well-timed genuine framing of their problems and weaknesses.

My Proudest Achievement

Tell me about the proudest achievement of your life. (This question fits in comfortably in the problem-free talk in an initial session)

Example Conversation

"Tell me about the most proud achievement of your life"
"When I helped my dad fix up his motorbike."

"Wow! How come you decided to help your dad with his motorbike?"
"I like putting things together and I like being with my dad. It's quiet too and I don't smoke so much."

"So you like putting things together and you enjoy being with your dad. Your dad must be a great bloke. I noticed too you want to smoke less - that's great!"

NOTE:

From this short exchange we have information about this student which we will be able to capitalize on later, should we deem it appropriate. We know:

- He likes to put things together (of a mechanical nature).

- He enjoys his father's company.

- He wants to smoke less.

- He enjoys 'Quiet' times.

Cheerleading

Example Conversation

"What's different since I last saw you?"
"I'm back in all my lessons."

"Wow! Last time I saw you were in the referral unit now you're in school full-time. That's fantastic! How did you manage that?"
"I've just been doing as the teachers ask first time, I've been getting my work done, I've been getting to lessons on time and I am keeping my hands off other students."

"That's amazing. How come you've achieved so much in 2 weeks? Doing as the teachers ask first time, getting your work done, getting to lessons on time and keeping your hands to yourself. That's a massive achievement in 2 weeks. I'm really impressed with you."
"Well, I was allowed out of the referral unit into a few lessons at first and I really enjoyed being back with everyone. So, I reckoned if I wanted to get out of the unit completely I'd have to do what everyone else was doing - so I just did"

Homework

The aim of Homework is to give the student a task that will support the actions a student has said they will execute.

There are several types of homework. The following are the ones I found to be very effective.

Homework 1

At the end of a session when a student has agreed to change certain behaviours, the counsellor might ask the student to:
"Notice the times when things are going well and acknowledge them."

Homework 2

After a session when a student has reported successes, the teacher/counsellor might ask the student to:
"Keep doing what you are doing. It is obviously working for you."

Homework 3

When a student has said they want to change a behaviour, the teacher/counsellor supports them by telling them to:
"Toss a coin. If it is Heads, you have to do what you said you were going to do. If it is Tails, you can do the action if you want to, but you don't have to."

The difference between a flowergirl and a princess is not how she acts, but how she is treated.

The Solution Focus Picture Sequence Exercise

This is an extremely powerful tool that is especially useful with younger students or those who find it difficult to put their thoughts into words.

The teacher explains to the student that she is going to ask a series of 'interesting' questions and that the student should illustrate their response as best they can. It should be made clear to the student that they are in a safe place and that they can draw whatever they feel they need/want to.

Some students ask if they can write their answers. It is acceptable to write the answers, especially when some students feel they cannot draw.

I have provided an example of a grid with the 'interesting' questions written in.

- The student is given a grid with six equal squares.
- He is told to number them 1 – 6, from left to right.
- The teacher then asks the following questions, reminding the student of the advice above.

1. In whatever way you can, draw the thing that you would like to get better, change.

2. Now, think of a super hero who you would like to help you sort out the problem. The super hero could be a friend, family member, pet, teacher, pop star,

film star. Whoever you want it to be, whoever you think you can trust.

3. Now, draw a picture showing you and the super hero meeting to sort out the problem.

4. Draw a picture showing how you would feel when the problem disappears for five minutes.

5. Draw a picture showing what your life will look like when the problem has gone completely.

6. Draw a picture of you thanking the superhero or giving them a gift for helping you.

Note:

It is important to tell the student that he/she can draw whatever she wants and that you or anyone else will not be asking him/her to explain the drawings.

The drawing can then remain the property of the student or be taken away by you to put on the student's file. I have never had a student who wants to keep the pictures - they always offer them to me to pin on my wall at my desk.

The problem	Superhero to help me with the problem
Superhero and me meeting	What life looks like for a little while without the problem
What life looks like when the problem is gone completely	Me thanking the Superhero

1 The problem	2 Superhero to help me with the problem
3 Superhero and me meeting	4 What life looks like for a little while without the problem
5 What life looks like when the problem is gone completely	6 Me thanking the Superhero

The problem	Superhero to help me with the problem
Superhero and me meeting	What life looks like for a little while without the problem
What life looks like when the problem is gone completely	Me thanking the Superhero

A Word about Multi-agency Meetings without a Solution Focus Approach.

Without a Solution Focus practitioner present I have always found these meetings left a slightly disappointing taste in the mouth. I have often sat in these meetings and counted the number of professionals in the room and concluded that their presence amounts to a lot of money. There could be all of the following in the meeting: paediatrician, school nurse, educational psychologist, social worker, an SEN Support Teacher from the local Children's Services - and the list goes on.

I have also found it sad that the parents and students are sometimes left feeling like the 'bad guys', the people with problems. There is an endless list of what has gone wrong with the family, then time is spent with the professionals deciding what someone amongst them can do next to help this poor family sort themselves out. Of course, these intentions are good and the professionals really are hoping that something they suggest will work.

The Non-Solution Focus Multi-agency Meeting

Present:

- Deputy Headteacher
- Youth worker
- Parent (dad)
- Behaviour Support Teacher (from the local Children's Services)
- Head of Year
- The student.

Deputy Head Teacher: We've called this meeting today to review Wayne's first 2 weeks in school in Year 9. As we all know, Wayne came to us having been excluded permanently from his last school. Well, I've got his report here and it doesn't look too good. There have been incidents in most of his lessons and some teachers won't have him in the room.

Head of Year: Yes, Wayne has had to come to me on several occasions, when teachers have struggled to keep him in the room. It's been a difficult 2 weeks.

Youth Worker: Wayne has attended some of the sessions with us, but I know he's missed a few and he has broken one of the rules of his ASBO by not being at home before 9 o'clock.

Deputy Head: Mr. Linden (Wayne's dad), we're trying everything but seem to be getting nowhere. We think the next step is for Wayne to go on a part-time time-table, where he say, comes in just 3 days a week. Wayne is disruptive and has little respect for himself let alone others. We can't allow him to continue causing mayhem in school.

Mr Linden: (Almost in tears), I've tried my best. I've taken away his Playstation, banned him from TV, but nothing works. I can't hit him anymore 'cos he's bigger than me now. This wasn't the way I brought him up. I tried to teach him good manners and how to behave.

Behaviour Support Teacher: I could offer some Anger Management sessions with Wayne one of the 3 mornings he'll be in school.

Deputy Head: Thanks, that might be useful. We'll look at putting a shortened timetable together for him at the end of this meeting. Wayne would you like to say something?

Wayne: Naw, only it's not all my fault, the teachers hate me 'cos they think I'm bad 'cos I've been excluded and they have no respect for me, so I have no respect for them.

Mr Linden: You should respect the teachers and do what they tell you to do. I'm gonna have to take time off work now to make sure you keep out of trouble on your 2 days out of school. That's more stress for me and less money. The boss ain't gonna like it. I could lose my job.

Wayne: You don't have to stay home with me. I can look after myself.

Mr Linden: You CAN'T look after yourself: You're in trouble with the Law and the teachers can't control you.

Deputy Head: Time's running short, the next lesson will be starting soon. Let's start putting together this shortened time-table.

The time-table is worked out and the Deputy Head thanks everyone for coming.

The outcomes of this meeting:

- It is established that Wayne isn't doing well in school.
- He's not attending all his YOT sessions.
- He's breaking his ASBO agreement.
- Dad doesn't know what to do to help his son.
- Dad has to take time off work.
- Wayne thinks the teachers don't like him.
- Wayne is put on a shortened time-table.

The Solution Focus Multi-Agency Meeting

Present:

- Deputy Head Teacher
- Youth Worker
- Parent (dad, Mr Linden)
- Behaviour Support Teacher (from Local Children's Service)
- Head of Year
- Student

Deputy Head: Thank you all for coming today. Can I thank Mr. Linden especially, because I presume you've had to take time off work. That also tells us how keen you are to support your son in moving forward. When I look through Wayne's report I see that there are some good comments in Food Technology, Drama and Art. Well done Wayne. You must be pleased, Mr Linden, that Wayne is making some progress.

Mr Linden: Yeah, but I want him to do well all the time, so he can get on and get a good job. I just want him to be happy.

Behaviour Support Teacher: I understand how you feel Mr Linden, as parents we all want the best for our children. When my teenager gets a bad letter home I feel really disappointed. Wayne, I'd like to speak to you for a moment. It's great that you're doing well in Food, Drama and Art.

What's different in these lessons?

Wayne: You get to do things with your hands and you can use your imagination a lot. In Drama I like pretending to be other people and putting on different voices.

Youth Worker: So, you like Drama, you know we run a Drama club on Thursdays and were hoping to put on a show later in the year. I'll talk to you about that later in the week when I see you. Perhaps we can look at building up your time with us through Drama and even Art.

Head of Year: So Wayne, what would have to happen in the other lessons for things to get as good as they are in Food, Art and Drama?

Wayne: I'd understand the work better, the teachers would help me more and I'd stop messing about.

Head of Year: Wayne, how much do you want things to improve in these other lessons? On a scale of 0 - 10, 0 being not at all, I can't be bothered and 10 being I want total improvement - where would you put yourself on this scale?

Wayne: 8

Behaviour Support Teacher: Wow! You want to improve that much! How come?

Wayne: Because I like it here in this school and I don't want to get excluded again. I hate getting into trouble, but sometimes I find the work too hard and I mess around, then the teachers shout at me and disrespect me in front of everyone, so I shout back at them. I don't want to get into trouble because I want to make my dad happy.

BSS Teacher: What else?

Wayne: I'll like going to lessons.

YOT Worker: What else?

Wayne: I'll feel good about myself 'cos I'll probably be getting letters home saying I'm doing well, then my dad will be proud of me.

BSS Teacher: Wow! You want your dad to be proud of you.

Wayne: Yes.

BSS Teacher: How will you know your dad's proud of you?

Wayne: He'll say, "nice one Wayne" and he might give me extra pocket money or a treat.

Deputy Head: Is that right dad? You'll say, "well done, and treat him?"

Mr Linden: Exactly right. I get a real buzz when I hear good things about him then I just want to give him everything.

Deputy Head (to Wayne): How certain are you that you can make these things happen in the classroom? 0 = I can't. 10 = pretty certain I can.

Wayne: 10

Deputy Head: Wow! That's high. How come?

Wayne: Because I'm already doing it in some lessons.

Deputy Head: Wayne, I'm really impressed with how keen you are to do well. I'd like you to start putting into practice the things you said you'd do as soon as you leave this meeting. I'd like you to drop by my office at the end of the week. Thank you all for coming, I'm sure you'll all agree that the meeting was very productive.

After the meeting, the BSS teacher suggests to the Deputy Head Teacher that Wayne is tested for a Specific Learning Disability such as Dyslexia, which could be causing him to disengage in lessons.

Outcomes of the meeting

- The Deputy Head uses the opportunity to thank the parent and to acknowledge how much he must care for his son.

- Wayne is praised for his progress in some areas.

- The adults present capitalise on Wayne's success and look at how they can make this happen more.

- Wayne gets the opportunity to show he cares for his dad.

- Dad gets the opportunity to express just how well he wants Wayne to do and how happy it makes him feel.

- Some of Wayne's strengths are discovered such as his love of Art and Drama and thus his creativity.

- Wayne will be tested for Dyslexia.

- Good relationships are established between parent and school staff.

- Wayne is given the opportunity to behave well in more lessons.

- There is an atmosphere of hope and possibilities in the room.

- Wayne is given an opportunity to imagine how the teachers would treat him when he is behaving well.

Becoming a Solution Focus fluent school

Imagine an institution where the people are exposed frequently to the language of Solution Focus. In my mind this would be an institution where individuals flourished and there would be an atmosphere of possibilities and hope; a place where the individual would feel safe - emotionally, intellectually and spiritually.

Perhaps that place does not yet exist and indeed may never completely exist. We can, however, work towards it.

Imagine a school whose students are frequently exposed to the language of Solution Focus...I know that to every one of you reading this a particular type of school will spring to mind. To some of you it will be the school in the leafy suburbs, to others it will be the tough inner city school, for some people it may even be the Pupil Referral Unit catering for permanently excluded pupils. Some of you may be thinking of Primary Schools. Whatever type of school sprang to mind, Solution Focus can support that school to improve.

How Will You Do It?

I would recommend that all adults in the school undergo a basic course in Solution Focus Brief Therapy. There are various agencies that offer this training, the most well-known of which is Brief, in London.

Once all staff in the school have been trained in the Method then the staff as a body could work together on its fluency and what it would look like.

Keep it Simple

Facets of the Method could be introduced slowly, making sure that it is understood and used by all staff.

For example, for students, who are consistently not handing in homework on time, staff could ask the question: you must have a very good reason for not handing your homework in, what is it? Once the reason has been established the student and teacher can work on a solution. As is frequently the case, giving a punishment (such as detention) may not solve the problem and could result in life becoming more difficult for the student and indeed for the teacher - a child in detention is a teacher in detention.

It also allows the teacher some insight into what might be going on in the student's world. It could be that the student may require some pastoral input because of problems at home. Not doing homework might simply be the warning light to school that school and home need to communicate and finding out the very good reason for homework not being done could allow this to happen.

Give the Method a high profile and attach significance and importance to it by appointing someone in charge of its implementation and sustainment. I would also suggest that this person has a senior role in school, which would send a clear message to staff about how highly the Senior Leadership Team values the Method as a tool for supporting the school ethos.

Before beginning to implement a 'Fluency in Solution Focus Policy' in school, it would be beneficial to review the school ethos with all staff. The solution focused method will enhance any school ethos and enhance further an already positive school ethos.

Being a school fluent in Solution Focus essentially means that the adults there believe in looking for solutions - the school is solution-oriented. It promotes an atmosphere of possibilities, the school is forward-looking.

How Will You Do It? 2

When we say a person is fluent in a language, we mean they speak that language with ease, because they have spoken it so much and know it so well. This is the sense in which I describe a school as being fluent in Solution Focus - the method is used with ease and fluidity by all and not just a few select members, who use it in certain situations. In most schools it is usually the pastoral staff who might use the Solution Focus Method (and other types of counselling) when running sessions with students. Staff such as Learning Mentors, School Counsellors, and the Connexions Advisor, for example. In the Solution Focus fluent school, the Method is used 'on the hoof' at every level.

Example: (in a solution focus school) - Adults to pupils:

A teacher encounters a student around school. The teacher knows that this student has been experiencing problems in a particular lesson (Humanities). The conversation the two have might go something like this:

"Hi Ben. How are things improving in Humanities?"
"O.K. Sir."

"Tell me a little more."
"I'm getting my work done sir and not being cheeky."

"That's great. How are you managing to get your work done and remain polite? That's been hard for you in the past."

"I just go in, get my book from the cupboard and start the quiz from the board, then I stop and listen to Miss when she's ready to start. I don't sit with my friends anymore."

"That's great! I'm really pleased that you've decided to start working and being polite. It's working for you not being near your friends. That was a good move."

The conversation could end at this point or the teacher could continue with the questions. A useful tool at this juncture could be "Flagging the Minefield."

"What if you find yourself beginning to miss the fun of being near your friends or they start sitting closer to you?"

"It was my decision to move away sir 'cos I'm doing well everywhere else and it's only in Humanities that I used to sit with Karl and Robbie. I see them at break and lunch sir. Anyway, I don't want to get anymore detentions because in Humanities they are on a Thursday and I don't want to miss any more footie practices."

Depending on how much time the teacher and student have the teacher might enquire how the student's getting on with football and inquire after how the student's own team is doing - whether it be Chelsea, Leyton Orient etc.

Notice how the teacher has concentrated only on what has been achieved and is improving and not on anything that's gone wrong. If, however, the student did talk about things going wrong, this teacher would then have the opportunity to further explore the student's resources to find out;

1. How the student managed to stop things from getting any worse
2. How does the student manage to keep things going well in similar situations in school or similar situations in the past:

"Things haven't been going well in Humanities. I've already had 2 detentions in 2 weeks."

"So, how have you kept things from getting any worse in Humanities?"
"I always do my homework and get it in on time."

"What else?"
"I always arrive on time."

"So, On a scale of 0 - 10, 0 being things are the worst they can be in Humanities and where 10 is things are fantastic, where would you place yourself on this scale at the moment?"
"5"

"That's quite high, so what are you doing already to put yourself on this 5?"
"Well, as I've said, I do my homework and get it in on time and I'm punctual."

"So how will you know you've moved up to a 6?"
"I won't be talking so much in class and not being silly with my mates."

"What will you be doing instead?"
"I'll be concentrating and getting on with my work."

"What's 1 small step you might take to start achieving that?"

"I'll sit away from all my friends next lesson 'cos I started to sit near Robbie again."

Earlier in this manual we looked at the Multi-agency meetings and saw that when conducted in a Solution Focused manner the process is more likely to lead to better outcomes for all concerned.

In the same manner, all other school meetings will benefit from being run using the Solution Focus Method. Let us look at a Year Team Meeting.

The Year Team Meeting

This will usually consist of;

- The form teachers in the year group
- The Head of Year, and
- Any other staff appropriate to the year group such as Learning Mentors, Achievement Co-ordinators etc.

In my experience, the Year Manager normally announces the agenda. Some of this agenda will simply be dissemination of information and some of it will look at how certain projects are progressing; problems within the year group, for example. Solution Focus comes into its own in this area;

- Measuring progress, and
- Looking at where and how further progress can be made.

Projects: this may be a project to look at a particular area such as behaviour, school uniform, homework etc.

Look at the following exchange in a Year Team Meeting.

"So, what's going well in our attempt to have all students wearing full school uniform at all times?"
"I've not had to tell anyone to change out of their trainers into their shoes and most students have their top buttons done up."

"What else?"
"The students don't seem shocked anymore when you remind them about uniform."

"So, where would you say we are in terms of success when 0 = we're failing and 10 = we're there?"
"7.5 (consensus)"

"That's fantastic. That's really high. I've noticed it myself as I walk around that it almost seems like a different school. I can't remember seeing so much bottle green for ages. How have you managed to do it, do you think?"
"By reminding them firmly yet politely when they aren't doing something right"

"By giving them unexpected house points for being smart."
"By having the 'Borrow an item of Uniform' shop open at all times so that they can't claim they haven't got one."

"So, how would we know we've moved up to 8.5?"
"More of them will be wearing their shoes."

"What else?"
"More will have their top buttons done up and their shirts tucked in."

In this particular case, the teachers felt that they wanted to be certain that what they had achieved was sustainable. They decided, therefore, that they would know they had reached 8.5 if the current level of uniform wearing could be maintained for a half-term using the methods they had talked about in the meeting.

Group Solution Focus Sessions

These are a very effective way of achieving positive change quickly and creating a group support atmosphere.

The majority of students I have worked with in these situations have benefitted greatly and in fact have wanted the sessions to continue beyond their sell-by dates.

At one school, the head teacher was so pleased with the change in the students' outlook and behaviour that he attended the next set of group sessions in order to learn the method for himself so that he could run the groups himself.

I always ask schools to provide me with a member of staff, who can sit in on the sessions to keep an eye on behaviour so that my sole role is as therapist - it's comforting for students to know that you are not going to tell them off.

I usually ask the adult sitting in on the session to have a card for each student and just to note any ratings and scalings for each student.

At the end of the session, each student looks into a hand-held mirror and makes a promise about a behaviour that they will attempt to change over the coming week/fortnight.

It is important to remember that if a student finds it impossible to look into the mirror that they do not have to do it. They will do it in their own time over the weeks, with encouragement from the other students and yourself. Some students over the course of the 5 sessions don't manage to do it, or hold it at the sides of their faces without actually looking at themselves.

How will you know?
What will you be doing?

Class/group Solution Focus Sessions for students experiencing behaviour difficulties in school.

First Session

- Ground rules established.
- Group leader introduces themselves and tells a little to the group about themselves.
- Each group member is given an opportunity to tell the rest of the group a little about themselves. Favourite football team, favourite music, clothes, person (super hero), colour etc.
- Students are asked where on a scale of 1 - 10 their commitment is to improving things.
- Students are asked to identify what their behaviour would look like if by magic the problems disappeared.
- Students are asked who would notice and what they would see as different in them once the problem had disappeared.
- Each member responds to this question while other members can contribute to what they would see each member doing differently.
- Each student says where they are on a Scale of 0 - 10 around the behaviours they just described above. 0 = doing none of them and 10 = doing it all the time.

- Students are asked what has caused them to rate themselves at a particular number.

- Students are then asked how they will know they have moved up a little on the scale.

- They are asked who will notice.

- The student then makes a promise to himself in front of the whole group and a mirror about the things they would do to move up one point on the scale.

How will you know?
What will you be doing?

Second and four subsequent sessions

- Students are surveyed concerning improvements since their last meeting.

- Group members are encouraged to describe things they have noticed were better about the behaviour of each of the other members during the week.

- They are then asked to rate themselves on the 0 - 10 scale.

- This is then followed by cheerleading and detailing how members made the changes.

- Students reflect on the effects their improved behaviours had on others and on themselves. If reported ratings regress, students are supported for their efforts to prevent their scores from going even lower, and they are asked what they would do differently next time to move higher up on their scales.

- Members discuss new promises they would like to make to themselves that would raise their ratings one more place on the scale.

- Students return to the mirror to make promises to themselves.

- Before the meeting concludes, members are asked to share with each other the improvements they have seen and expect to continue to see in one another.

- The group is then dismissed.
- Sessions three through six follow the same format (if school feels the sessions need to continue).

Exercise

Find the Solution Focus Tools in the following Sessions.

Session 1.

"What would have to happen after these sessions for you to think they were successful?"
"I wouldn't be getting into so much trouble."

"What would be happening instead?"
"I'd be getting on with my work, staying out of trouble. The teachers would see me as a good student."

"What difference will it make to you when the teachers start seeing you as a good student?"
"No difference."

"How would you know the teachers are seeing you as a good student?"
"They would try and stop people from disrupting me. They'd give me another chance if I did something wrong."

"You go to bed and overnight something wonderful happens. You didn't cause it to happen, but when you wake up you know your life is exactly as you want it. Describe this wonderful day."
"Breakfast in bed - it's fried food, chips, bacon, cold drink and a piece of fresh fruit. All my clothes would be laid out ready for me to go to school. First lesson PE, big match on

the field, everyone has their kit. In English I've got all my course work done. IT is ok, I wouldn't change it. I enjoy Art, I wouldn't change that either. I'm getting on well with a specific teacher. She stays out of my way. Chips in the dining hall at lunch are hot."

"Where would you rate your behaviour at the moment? 0 awful and 10 = excellent."
"7"

"That's quite high. How come?"
"I stay in quite a few of my lessons, it's just one subject, Maths, that's a problem."

"How possible is it for you to do something about this situation in Maths? 0 = impossible and 10 = very possible."
"6. If I really did try I could change things. I could work my way into this teacher's good books, get my head down."

"What difference will it make to her?"
"I don't know but I've done it before. I was doing well."

"What difference will your improved behaviour make to the teacher?"
"She'll try and aggravate me."

"What difference would it make to you if she didn't aggravate you?"
"I'd be in the class and learning more with better grades."

"What difference would this make to your relationship with her?"
"She wouldn't accuse me so much."

"Just suppose you have been accused wrongly of, doing something in class with this teacher and she is shouting at you. How are you going to keep on top of this situation?"
"I'll do my best not to get angry. I'll remain as composed as I can and say it wasn't me."

"What else?"
"Stay calm."

"How will you manage to stay calm?"
"Think about something else."

"When was a time when you were last in a situation when you could have lost your temper but you didn't?"
"In football on Saturday. I was fouled badly. I was going to hit the boy."

"How did you manage not to hit him?"
"I thought about other people, like how it's going to affect the team. I just thought I shouldn't get worked up over it because it's not worth it."

"What difference will the improvements make to your mum?"
"She'll be happy."

"How will you know she's happy?"
"I'll just know."

"What difference will this make to you?"
"I'd concentrate more."

Exercise

Find the solution focus tools in the following sessions.

Session 2.

All about the student:

Favourite Food: Lasagne and chips.

Favourite pop star: Jamelia

Favourite film: I know what you did last summer

Favourite subject in school: English

Favourite colour: Pink and lilac.

Ambition: Nurse.

"What's changed since you knew I was coming to see you?"
"I've started being quieter in lessons."

"How have you managed to do that?"
"I've just wanted to get on well."

"What would have to change for you to feel it was worth seeing me?"
"My behaviour."

"What would be different about your behaviour?"
"I'd be quiet like I used to be."

"What else?"
"I wouldn't fight so much."

"What would you be doing instead?"
"I'd be with my sister in year 8."

"What else would be different?"
"I'd hang around with people who I wouldn't get into trouble with."

"On a scale of 0 - 10, how keen are you to make some changes for the better? 0 = Forget it, I'm not interested and 10 = I would really like to do it."
"9"

"Wow! That's high, you're really keen. How come it's so high?"
"I'm not really fighting and I'm getting a bit quieter"

"When isn't there a problem?"
"Sometimes when I'm at home and sometimes when I'm at school."

"When things are good at school, what's different?"
"I wait for my sister in reception and don't get to see the people I bully."

"When things are going well at home, what's different?"
"I'm doing my thing and she's doing hers."

"You must have a very good reason for bullying, what is it?"
"I get bullied and sometimes the people I bully get on my nerves a lot."

"What difference would it make to you if these girls who get on your nerves kept away from you?"
"I would probably be doing other things with my sister such as walking 'round school and we might go to the library, instead of trying to deal with Jessica."

"You must have a very good reason for bullying Jessica, what is it?"
"She's butting into my business."

"How are you going to achieve this 9?"
"I'm going to stay away from Jessica and go to Drama with my sister."

"Imagine everywhere you go Jessica is there and she's looking at you and butting in, which annoys you. How are you going to manage not to respond to her?"
"I can tell the teacher she's winding me up. I'll walk away with my sister. I'm going to get people who are around me to help me keep my cool."

"When these changes in your behaviour start happening, what difference will it make to your teachers?"
"They'll be pleased that I'm managing the situation and not allowing Jessica to get to me."

"How will you know the teachers are pleased?"
"They'll say, 'well done' at the end of the lesson."

"What difference will these improvements make to your dad?"

"He'll know that I'm not getting into trouble because my reports are good and he'll be happy."

"How will you know he's happy?"

"I'll be getting pocket money and treats."

Possible Answers - in order of appearance in the interview.

Session 1.

- What would have to happen...?
- What difference...?
- Miracle Question...
- Scaling - where would you rate your behaviour...?
- What difference?
- Just Suppose
- What else?
- How, what, where, when?
- How, what, where, when?
- How, what, where, when?
- How, what, where, when?
- How, what, where, when?
- How, what, where, when?
- What difference?

Session 2.

- How, what, where, when?
- How, what, where, when?
- How, what, where, when?
- How, what, where, when?
- How, what, where, when?
- How, what, where, when?
- Scaling
- Cheerleading
- How, what, where, when?
- How, what, where, when?
- You must have a very good reason...?
- How, what where, when?
- You must have a very good reason
- How, what where, when?
- Flagging the Minefield
- How, what, where, when/what difference?
- How, what, where, when?
- What difference?
- How, what, where, when?

I hope you enjoy doing these exercises. They are somewhat simple, and I have made them so to demonstrate to the reader how a simple conversation can lead to such effective change.

Finally and Simply...

It is important to notice that in all the conversations demonstrated in this book, the student is given the opportunity to put into words what they imagine their future behaviour or actions to be. They are then assisted to decide how they are going to make these behaviours or actions a reality.

This is why the method is called Solution Focused Brief Therapy.

37388305R00061

Made in the USA
Middletown, DE
26 February 2019